ANDALUSIAN DAWN

ANDALUSIAN DAWN

Poems by Nick Carbó

Cherry Grove Collections

Published by Cherry Grove Collections
P.O. Box 541106
Cincinnati, OH 45254-1106

ISBN: 1932339442
LCCN: 2003117101

Poetry Editor: Kevin Walzer
Business Editor: Lori Jareo

Typeset in Copperplate and American Garamond BT by WordTech
Communications LLC, Cincinnati, OH

Visit us on the web at www.cherry-grove.com

ACKNOWLEDGMENTS

The author would like to gratefully acknowledge the Fundacíon Valparaíso in Mojácar, Spain for a series of residencies which inspired these poems and provided the necessary support to sustain them in their production. To the Corporation of Yaddo, the MacDowell Colony, the New York Foundation for the Arts and the National Endowment for the Arts for fellowships which came at a critical time in the writing of these poems. He would also like to thank the following poets and critics for their generous support: Michael Collier, Terrance Hayes, Crystal Williams, Edward Hirsch, Thomas E. Kennedy, Brooks Haxton, Elisabetta Marino, and Rocio Davis.

Thanks to the editors of the following publications in which these poems first appeared:

5 A.M. "Directions to My Imaginary Childhood" and "Typhoon Signal
    No. 1"
Big City Lit: "Ay! Que Dolo!"
Columbia Poetry Review: "Dulzura," "Mis Versos," and "Pelos"
DisOrient: "Serena" and "La Comarca"
Folio: "Telling Ancient Visayan Time"
Gargoyle: "Translating Lorca in Andalusia" and "Tormenta

Electromagnetico"

Gulfstream!ng: "Mal Agueros" and "Capis Windows"

Indiana Review: "Marlene Dietrich's Filipino Butler Finds this Note and Begins to Suspect she is a German Spy" and "Consequences"

Luna: "Fuente" and "Mujer"

Poetry: The following poems are copyrighted in 1996 by The Poetry Foundation, and reprinted by permission of the Editor of *Poetry:* "Carta de Umm Al-Hákam para Ben Quzman" July 1996, "Carta de Ben Quzman Para Umm Al-Hákam" July 1996, and "Respuesta de Umm Al-Hákam" July 1996.

Poetry New York: "Parejas"

Poet Lore: "Viento" and "Humedad"

TriQuarterly: "Eras del Lugar," "El Camino," and "Amor Con Agua" under the title of "Mojacar Love Poem"

The following poems first appeared in these anthologies:

A Habit of Shores (University of Philippines Press, 1999): "Robo"

The Breadloaf Anthology of New American Poets (Middleburry College Press, 2000): "Robo" and "Verso Libre"

Humor Me: An Anthology of Humor by Writers of Color (University of Iowa Press, 2002): "Grammarotics"

Tigertail: A South Florida Poetry Annual (Tigertail Productions, 2003): "Gather Like Soldiers" and "Slow Song"

For

Athena
Bianca
and
Chad

CONTENTS

Un día, con el alba, volvía solitario

de mis cosas de hombre. Pudo ser hace tiempo.

La claridad nacía del fondo de las calles

como la pena nace del fondo de una copa.

—Rafael Guillén

THE EVENING'S SILVER IN ANDALUSIA

.

ROBO

"Was Andalusia here or there? On the land . . . or in the poem?"

—Mahmoud Darwish

I must admit to this outright theft.
Before the crickets could impede me,

I reached outside my window
to grab as much of Andalusia as

I could in the palm of my hand.
I took the evening's silver

from the olive trees, the yellow slumber
from the lemons, the recipe for gazpacho.

I made a small incision in my heart
and slipped in as much as my left

and right ventricles could hold.
I reached for a pen and a piece of paper

to ease-out the land into this poem.

I closed the small incision in my heart

and closed the wooden shutters

of my window.

ERAS DEL LUGAR

—for Beatrice

is the name of this little known dirt road
that leads to the Rio de Aguas.
"The place where one thrashes"
trigo trechel, tremesino, marzal,
candeal, piche, jeja, or *blanquillo.*
Joselito and his burro have rounded
the corner with a bale of saracen wheat.
These are the flat stones where all
the farmers of the *lugar* have thrashed
their harvests for centuries.
Joselito nudges his burro to unload—
Aya, Negrita. Ya estamos.
Antonio Maria is leading his herd of goats
to the dry river bed at the end of the road.
He sings *guajiras* to all his goats—

Adios pueblo de Mojácar,
adios pueblo de alegría,
cuantas penas y miserías
me recorro de memoría . . .

17

Joselito takes his pitch-fork

carved from bleached olive wood

and launches the dry wheat-stalks

into the air. Tomorrow morning,

the scent of fresh-baked bread will

pass by every window of this little known

dirt road and Antonio Maria will return

with his herd of goats singing—

. . . Yo alli que tenía
mi recreo y mi dulzura
divirtiéndome como mozo
y ahora me veo así
preso en un calabozo.

TRANSLATING LORCA IN ANDALUSIA

Take the word *salitre* and look
under blue rocks for its true meaning.
To find *la luz de la cañavera*
go to the dry riverbed towards
nightfall and lay still for an hour.
To be entertained by *arañas titiriteras*,
light up a cigarette and sing a *saeta*
to the easternmost wall of your house.

You must ask Fernando "el Manitas" to
Líbrame del suplicio
de verme sin toronjas.
He has the right set of teeth
and number of bronze tools for the job.
To see the *mariposas negras*, locate
the moonless night in a grove
of olive trees and clap your hands.

VERSO LIBRE

In this white room in Mojácar,
I wait for the potato of tears

that will arrive in an ordinary
wheel barrow when news

of the death of a family member
spurts through the phone. Five-thirty

and the Andalusian cocks begin
their newspaper routes.

I can read all the signs—
the odor of disturbing dreams,

the umber-spotted lizard on the wall,
the sound of the waning moon.

I have to write it all down
in this white room in Mojácar.

HUMEDAD

On a humid night like this—
olive leaves turn silver,
air is as still as a statue of a saint,
mosquitos come out with their neumatic tools
to drill for four thousand red blood cells.

On a humid night like this—
figs on the fig trees shake their bellies
and laugh their way into a purple ripeness,
the farmer's young wife down the dirt road slaps
a mosquito on her naked thigh.

AMOR CON AGUA

—for Denise

As we walk along the dry river bed of Rio de Aguas,
I think of basket-weaving whispers around
your all-night hips. And now,

that the moon is almost full, I wonder if the tiny
bits of silver in the sand will catch
that midnight Moorish light.

On nights like these, the locals say
that the mountain of Mojácar la Vieja glows
when the moon is just right. The sounds

of the crickets, your foot steps,
your non-asthmatic inhales are also just right
for something to happen. So I follow

what the lost river says *give her a kiss
on the neck.* Your hair smells of the sea.
Removet her blouse, her skirt, her socks.

Your skin between your breasts
feel softer than the ripest olives from the groves
on that hill. *Kiss her from her toes*

up to her lips, up to her eyes.
Your hands on my bare thighs taste
better than a whole plate of membrillo—

we roll around on the fine soil
of the river bed, our bodies begin to sparkle
with tiny bits of silver.

Our nude bodies are glowing
like the mountain of Mojácar la Vieja
which is also glowing.

EL CAMINO
—for Bibi and Ulrich

The walk down from the *Taller Electrico* sign

is somewhat more steep now that they have paved

the first hundred meters of the initial incline—

we say this as if we've been in Mojácar

long enough to see significant change—

missing the dust, the flattened goat droppings,

and even the boulders that used to frame

our feet—now Ulrich says the new

pavement absorbs the heat and melts

the soles of his shoes—*progress is simply terrible!*

Bibi has written a story-book for their grandchildren

of that little-known dirt road—

two choices from the bottom of the first incline:

to the left—a grove of lemon trees, the sound

of water rushing by in irrigation canals,

the basement window where suddenly a pig-dog

or a white dog with a pink snout will leap up

and bark the breath out of your stride—

to the right—some white plaster houses and a pack

of dogs barking at you from above—*they smell*
the scent of children who've been bad.

After the Odyssean trials with the pig dog,
the dog-with-four-nostrils, the dogs whose growls
come from the sky, is another bend
with a cactus patch as big as a bus
where you can stand for one duro under
its airconditioned shade—then another steep
incline past two brick-stone-plaster-wood houses
across from each other where a family
of goats baa from behind closed doors,
and where a family of pigs oink out
their smelly town gossip—
a large happy palm tree with smiling leaves
greets you at the bottom of the hill—turn
left along a tall stone wall where the Moors
fought off the Barbary Pirates—more trees
with lemons dreaming their yellow dreams
on their green branches—further along
is a pomegranate tree with flowers
dancing flamencos in red dresses—again,
the sound of water running

to the terraced fields of fig trees further below—
lost sounds of Moorish children playing hide-and-seek.

A few more dusty half-turns and down
into a miniature canyon with seven-year growth
of wild plants scattered on the dry river bed—look
left—an old stone foot-bridge or what could be
a miniature Roman aqueduct—around noon,
a lonely tied-up white goat will *baa baa*
from under a thicket of leaves—rising
from the other side like Orpheus and Eurydice
in sneakers and *alpargatas*—we see the house
with one donkey, one white horse,
no cats, no dogs—a bend to the left
and the last steep hundred meters up
to the lively sounds of Antonio Maria's house
where we begin to sweat again
from our foreheads full of Andalusian sun.

VOLVER A EMPEZAR

Returning to begin again—
to begin with three periods

on the face of an Andalusian dog,
or are those fleas?

These images are being disassembled
by ants—alphabet ants

that won't stay as words,
that crawl off the page

to rejoin that parched landscape
outside my window.

I am beginning again.
Voices of the collective cactus patches

won't let me ramble
into a narrative frame of mind.

Those thorns are enough warning—
there is no time for long sentences,

there is not enough water in the valley,
there is not enough shade for metonomy.

Some women living near the dry river bed
still walk up to the fountain balancing

empty clay *jarros* on their heads—
come down the mountain

embracing their *jarros* on their hips
as if they were babies.

Every day they return to begin again.
As I must do with these words

before the ink dries in this dry wind,
before they rise and rejoin

that parched landscape
outside my window.

SONGS OF ANCIENT ARAB ANDALUSIA

MUJER

"It is not strange at all
That my desire
Was so excited.

When he sees water
A person thirsting
Thirsts the more."

—Al-Radi Bi-llah Razid (Ronda, 11th-12th c.)

That woman does not know

how many doors she has opened

in the city under my *almalafa*.

All my pores want to learn her name,

where she lives, who her father may be.

Is she new to Ronda?

What ornate wooden panels

have hidden her from us this long?

I would give bags of gold to be

a knot in that wood.

DULZURA

"Treat with sweetness the one that can cause you harm
and accompany him to the door of your house.

In this world all is an illusion.
You must fawn over the person you fear the most."
—Abu Utman S ad b. Luyun (1282-1349)

The one who could hurt me most

would be El Amin the butcher,

the finest cut of his blade

does not compare to how

he has been eyeing my wife

since the last night of Ramadan.

Tomorrow, I will bring him

a box of frankincense.

PELOS

"Heavens! Since the day that destiny has separated us,
my temples have turned gray!"
—Ali ibn Muhammad ibn Jatima, al-Ansari

I have white rabbits running around
my dreams at night. See the streaks
they leave on my temples? You! You put
them there so I would never forget
the lines of your face as you bent
to lick my belly button.

CARTA DE UMM AL-HÁKAM PARA BEN QUZMAN

"My messenger will come, receive him well,

If you can stoop to write a letter, then

I will break off a bone to be my pen,

And write with it, in blood, a fit reply."

> —Abu Bakr Muhammad ben Quzman (c. 1086-1160 A.D.)

So many harvests of oranges, of figs,

of saracen wheat, and now this—

you say you have lost your moon

because my hair does not caress your shoulders,

because I'm not there to bring you early light,

because I've taken my caravan to Moxacar.

Your memory is as short as a rabbit's tail.

Remember, it was you who would not listen

to the little birds in your heart, instead

you heeded the mathematics of your father,

of the old men in the mosque. You must stop

this foolish wind, I will not bubble under your breath.

CARTA DE BEN QUZMAN PARA UMM AL-HÁKAM

Your camphor scented letter came to Cordova
through dry cobbled streets—
as your words passed these white houses,
azaleas seemed to bloom.

It's true, my sweet Umm Al-Hákam, I see
everything from this terraced window, and now
I'm breaking off—*crack*—a bone,
as I said I would in reply.

RESPUESTA DE UMM AL-HÁKAM

Oh, Ben Quzman, you poor glum thing!
I do not sustain your city's azaleas.
I do not bring gentle rains to Cordova.
I do not yearn for your hands on my face.

What your eyes touch are just illusions.

And that little trick with bone and blood—
a pomegranate, a turtle dove feather.
My heart remains inside the walls of Moxacar.
My face now belongs to another poet's hands.

MIS VERSOS

"But my contemporaries are displeased with my prose
and my verses just like a sword is displeased being
in the sheath carried by a coward."
—Abd al Samad

They don't repeat my verses at the baths
or around the fountains in Almeria anymore.

My words had travelled by horse and donkey
as far as Cordoba, my phrases even pleased

the purple flowers of the Alhambra. A boy before
his manhood will never hear my Song to Sulaiman.

CLAVELES

You have made it to Al-myria
with only one casualty, a black horse

that was to be ridden by Ibn Al-Saud Sahwari
to his wedding. You are fortunate

as a morning dove out of reach of a cat's paws.

The bride has died of a sudden illness

and tomorrow they begin taking down
the blue and white banners, the red carnations.

EL HIJO DE IBN BEN-YAMIN

He is the eldest son
of the silver-smith Ibn Ben-Yamin.
I was looking for something to celebrate
my appointment as chief architect
of the new Alcazaba and I walked
into this little shop next to the bath houses.

Our hands only touched briefly
as he slipped a ring with rubies
on my finger. I must design a fountain
for the central patio that murmurs
his name day and night.

FUENTE

"How beautiful the fountain jet
   When it pelts the sky with momentary stars
That nimbly skip like acrobats . . ."

—Ben Raia (Sevilla, 13th c.)

Not even in Alexandria, Haifa, or Damascus

are the fountains as refreshing

as this one in Sevilla. Everybody comes here

to gather the latest word of which kingdom

has recently fallen. Was it a Christian

or Moorish king? Troubadors come

with their instruments and latest tales.

A favorite among the Christians of Sevilla

is a story about a mercenary named *El Cid.*

What can I say, the common people have always

been entertained by common tales.

Look, there's Ibn Khaldun, the historian

from Ceuta. He's with those old men sitting

by the shallow pool, debating

the positions of the stars. It's amazing how our world revolves around this fountain.

.

TORMENTA
ELECTROMAGNETICO

VIENTO

This Almeria wind has the strength to scare
even the most sturdy of souls,

viene en carcajadas—comes in fits of laughter,

with the clear intent of diamonds—

a thousand hands banging

every open window of this house.

TORMENTA ELECTROMAGNETICO

Did you hear the thrumming storm clouds
passing by Don Carmelo's house last night?

His donkeys started drawing maps to Nerja,
his goats put on their second-hand suits,

and all you could see were tiny
television sets swarming the property lines.

Within minutes they found me on my porch
and circled above my head, showing

me images of your face, your face watching
your husband's hands. I can't wait

to fax my string around your wrists, tie you
to my barometric bed and begin

a correspondence of our flesh. The sky will buzz
as you lick your guilty desires off my chest.

SERENA

Lai lai le le ay!

Busco la moon, la lunera

on the corner of ayer

in the decade of bad ideas.

Castigado for the castration

of sugar confessions en la bañera

da me un beso she said

dancing away with the slippery hose.

LA COMARCA

La *luz* of a thousand years
brimming in a glass of vino blanco,
my corner table en el Café del Caballo Rojo
asks for your *voz de verano.*

I lost my breath one evening
in Cuevas del Almanzora, un *plato*
cracked on the rim of midnight
donde quema el alma de Andalucia.

AY! QUE DOLO!

Dona Josefina has thrown my goat
out onto the calle El Fez—
Ay! The menu of pain is as big
as a queen-sized aha umbrella.

The lolita from the barrio chino licks
the sellos and then my luau—
there is a hint of ajo from Ab-derabad,
with periodos of adages and lapis lazuli.

I have known the fonda of Dona Josefina,
the jetty of her hips, under the veil
of her mild protests where pigs and lox
do mix in a yodel of ah-do-do-dah.

The lolita from the barrio chino is a rider
of net gains and bronze sea snakes—
she holds a baroque club in one hand
and ma of mana from a mouse in the other.

PAREJAS

If you kill a scorpion, its partner will come
looking for its mate is an old saying

of the gitanos of the Levante. I was careful
to include the whole body of that fat scorpion

and squeeze two hundred pounds on the leather sole
of my left shoe. In bed, I worry

about the partner I missed, the one
who is probably scurrying up the dirt road,

following my every other foot step
to the sixth house with three lighted

windows on the second floor. I imagine
a lethal stinger getting bigger and bigger,

filling with anger as it nears the scent
of the leather shoe and of the foot

that has killed its mate. All I see now
is just a giant stinger navigating

the black and white checkered tiles
of the first floor. I'm gripped

by that helpless fear in the faces
of the men in the movie *Jaws*

when they spot the fin of the great white shark
circling their sinking boat. I lift

the bed sheet—my wife's thigh warmly pressed
over mine. I caress the slope of her shoulder,

whisper in her ear *if anyone ever harms you,*
I'll track that person down. She responds

in mid-dream speech, *Yes, honey, we'll talk*
about it in the morning.

MAL AGUEROS

If you come to Mojacar
and peel open an orange full of worms,
count how many there are because
those are the days it will take for your body
to decompose after you are buried.

If you come to Mojacar
and find a small green snake with its back
broken, don't step on it or you'll cause
an earthquake that will catch up to you
while you sleep in a continent far, far away.

If you come to Mojacar
and two brown long-legged spiders crawl
on your face and shoulders, keep a sharp eye
out for two individuals, a mother-son, or
sister-sister who will try to take your money.

If you come to Mojacar
and see a scorpion scurry by your feet,

note the direction it ran to, north, south,

east, or west. You must avoid going there

or risk the sting of losing a loved one.

If you come to Mojacar

and a cock crows ten times at three

in the morning, lock your door and all

the wooden windows because nightmares in silver

dresses will arrive to slip into your bed.

DIRECTIONS TO MY IMAGINARY CHILDHOOD

DIRECTIONS TO MY IMAGINARY CHILDHOOD

If you stand on the corner

of Mabini Street and Legazpi Avenue,

wait for an orchid colored mini-bus

with seven oblong doors,

open the fourth door—

an oscillating electric fan

will be driving, tell her to proceed

to the Escolta diamond district—

you will pass Maneng Viray's Bar,

La Isla de los Ladrones book shop,

the Frederick Funston fish sauce factory,

and as you turn left into Calle de Recuerdos,

you will see Breton, Bataille, and Camus

seated around a card table playing

abecedarian dominoes—

roll down your window and ask

them if Mr. Florante and Miss Laura

are home, if the answer is, yes,

then proceed to Noli Me Tangere park

and wait for a nun named Maria Clara—

if the answer is, *Je ne se pas!*, then turn

right onto the parking lot of Sikatuna's

supermarket to buy a basketful

of lansones fruit, then get back

to Calle de Recuerdos until you reach

the part that's lined with tungsten-red

Juan Tamad trees, on the right will be

a house with an acknowledgments page

and an index, open the door and enter

this page and look me in the eye.

CAPIS WINDOWS

How do you enter that Manila
frame of mind, that woven
mat of noodle house restaurants,

that dawn of tapis tasting women,
that hankering of hourly hauntings?
Drive along Roxas Boulevard

when the moon has just clocked
out of third shift and the sea horses
are returning to their feeding stables.

Walk the afternoon trees of Taft Avenue
and talk to the mechanics of Sunday
medicine. Ask them for recipes

to cure fire-retardant love. Bask
in the baying of mahogany dogs on Mabini
street and pass through the red

wrought iron gates of Calle Remedios

where you'll find a house with capis windows

where Doña Inez waits to sew your skin.

TELLING ANCIENT VISAYAN TIME

There were more than a dozen names
for the sun dancing across the daylight hours—

nasirakna was the time of watching birds
from green dawn to blue dusk,

nabahadna was the sun climbing the face
of the sky past the nose, past the forehead,

iguritlogna was the time for the gossiping
hens to sit and lay their white eggs,

makalululu, was when the sun was so high
that your bracelets fell as you pointed to the sky,

natupongna sa lubi was the sun sinking past
the tops of red palm trees on the horizon,

apuna was the time when the sun hung
on the horizon's bed about to fall asleep

igsirinto was when it was too dark to recognize
the face of your uncle, sister, grandmother,

or child as they walked up to your house
in the cricket sound dark.

TYPHOON SIGNAL NO. 1

This is where the typhoon starts—
inside the fourth paragraph,
ten city blocks away,

where the neurosurgeon halfs
La Celestina, where you occupy
the spot under that Tiffany lamp,

where Edgar Rice Burroughs laughs,
where sugar cane is thigh
high, where you apply lipstick,

where the address numbers
are transposed, where hearts
take on airs of Parisian avenues,

where Mexican silver coins
are exchanged for salt, where
there is no fine line between art

and meteorology, where the big

gingerbread boy answers

to the name of Alfredo, where you

take that moment to adjust

to my poem, where the metaphor

escapes from your throat.

SPEECH IMPEDIMENTS

"I like dappled hats," she said
as she lit the incendiary device.

He enjoyed her wet diphthongs
on her nape, his frequency
modulator, his frenulum.

"You must warn me," she said
as she manipulated the milibars.

He was engulfed by the heat
of her cardamom mouth, her amplitude,
her guttural declensions.

GRAMMAROTICS

The angle of delight is best
achieved while rubbing

the pluperfect button
in tiny syllabic circles

while the glottal stop needs
firm accentual strokes

for copulative conjunction
to occur. The placement

of the preterite tense
at the entrance

of a lubricated sentence
assures the inevitable

apostophe. However,
if the apostrophe occurs

prematurely the result
is then a dangling

modifier, also
commonly known as

a pathetic fallacy.

MARLENE DIETRICH'S FILIPINO BUTLER FINDS THIS NOTE AND BEGINS TO SUSPECT SHE IS A GERMAN SPY

pick a feathered locomotive
from out of my matching amber hair

take it out for a walk along Harding
and Benchley Avenues on the sunny

side of the sidewalk, talk to no
one with titanium stares

or pig-iron shoes from Denmark
stop by 202 Jane Street and ask

for a poltergeist by this name_____
inform him of the charge' d'affaire's

sentence for treason for selling
camphor scented secrets to Chanel

GATHER LIKE SOLDIERS

The clouds gather like soldiers—
that metaphor is not new,
Aleximander of Kroton said it in 95 B.C.
just before he was struck
by lightning. And the great orator
Ibn Muhammad Saladin of Cordova in 1141 A.D.
pronounced the end of a seven-year drought
with that same image. In Russia
the poet Ludmila Kandourova used
the reverse—describing
the Red Army soldiers entering St. Petersburg
as thunder clouds—impossible to stop.

Why should I care if it rains
later this afternoon in this rose garden?
Tomorrow the roses will still be roses
and the clouds will continue releasing metaphors.

SLOW SONG

"It was such a night when it is good to hear from faraway,
across the dark fields, the slow song of a Negro on his way
to make love."

—Carson McCullers

I could not blame you for the word, *periphery*.

I could not take down the planets, the stars, the names

of constellations like ornaments from a Christmas tree.

I could not remove the smell of a million fireflies

burning rows and rows and rows between us.

CONSEQUENCES

". . . absolve me, even though you are but a stuffed bird."

—*Wislawa Szymborska*

I am also your grandmother's Hungarian silver broach,

your husband's embroidered handkerchief, your Aunt's

suede purse from Sofia, your cousin's parasol

from Venice, your father's pantaloons from Pantagruel,

your sister's tea cup from Delft, your nephew's caw,

your nephew who stole until you turned him into a bird.

Nick Carbó is the author of *El Grupo McDonald's* (1995) and *Secret Asian Man* (2000) which won the 4th Annual Asian American Literary Award. He has edited three anthologies of Philippine Literature: *Returning a Borrowed Tongue* (1996), *Babaylan* (2000), and *Pinoy Poetics* (2004). He also co-edited an anthology *Sweet Jesus* (2002) with Denise Duhamel. Among his awards are grants in poetry from the National Endowment for the Arts (1997) and New York Foundation for the Arts (1999), and residencies from Fundacíon Valparaíso (Spain), Le Chateau de Lavigny (Switzerland), the MacDowell Colony, and Yaddo.

Also by Nick Carbó

El Grupo McDonald's
Secret Asian Man

As editor and co-editor:

Returning A Borrowed Tongue: An Anthology of Filipino and
Filipino American Poetry
Babaylan: An Anthology of Filipina and Filipina American Writers
Sweet Jesus: Poems About the Ultimate Icon
Pinoy Poetics: A Collection of Critical and Autobiographical
Essays on Filipino Poetics

Printed in the United States
40084LVS00002B/6

9 781932 339444